NIDDERDALE YESTERDAY

Gouthwaite Reservoir

Nidderdale Yesterday

A Pictorial Record of Life in a Yorkshire Dale

David Alred

David Alred

Smith
Settle

First published in 2001 by
Smith Settle Ltd
Ilkley Road
Otley
West Yorkshire
LS21 3JP

ISBN   Paperback   1 85825 158 3
            Hardback   1 85825 159 1

British Library Cataloguing-in-Publication data:
A catalogue record for this book is available from the British Library.

Frontispiece: Gouthwaite Reservoir

Set in Usherwood

Designed, printed and bound by
SMITH SETTLE
Ilkley Road, Otley, West Yorkshire LS21 3JP

Contents

Acknowledgements

Many people have kindly permitted me to copy and use their photographs. They and others have helped in many ways, and I should like to record my gratitude to them all for their contributions:

Phyllis Stevenson, Robert Booth, Mary and Christine Houseman, Frances Stevenson, Jack Gill, Jean Blakey, Ken Lambert, Jane Newall, Freddy and Betty Wilson, John and Amelia Wilson, Ethel and Mary Dale, Barbara Houseman, Ruth Newbould, Peggy Lambert, Hilda Tuley, Frank Houseman, John Richmond, Eric Reynard, Hilda Walmsley, John Threadgold, Hilda Hollings, Kate and Mary Smith, Arthur Worsnop, John and Margaret Verity, Ken Nelson, Frances Simpson, David and Ruby Booth, Maurice Rispin, Roger Gill, Howard Wood, Wilf and Marjorie Bellerby, Bridget and Richard Verity, Dawn Bussey, Ann Kent, Patrick Gratton, Sue Clarke, Harold and Mary Atkinson, Ian and Brian Weatherhead, Audrey Summersgill, John and Alice Gurney, George Harrison, Jean Johnson, Biddy Brown, Pam Holliday, Jean Marshall, Stanley Walker, David Swindells, Ethel Mawer, Pam Garbutt, Shirley Dunwell, Gillian Harling, Kathleen Atkinson, Edwin Knightson, Joe and Margaret Stoney, Marion Longster, Jack Suttill, Daphne and Russel Grant, Margaret Hullah, Freddy, Mary and Christine Harker, Judith Hopkinson, Peter Wells, Kay Clark, Olive Dougill, Jack and Rita Hannam, Betty Brown, Freda Marsden, Dorothea and Norman Houseman, Joe Hardcastle, Josephine and George Carter, May Ainsley, Betty Whitaker, Janet Leeming, Janet Dinsdale, John and Mary Rayner, Dinah Lee, John Robson, Norman and Margaret Wellock, William and Doreen Verity, Lena Wilson, Matthew Brown, Ernest Pinkney, Gerald Simpson, Dorothy Furniss, George Gill, Gillian Furniss, Arthur Pickard, Peter Pullan, Chris Sexton, Ronny Layfield, Edith Harker, Joe Weatherhead, Christine Weatherhead, Rose Riley, Carolyn Hudson, Joan Harper, Muriel Imeson, Winny Newbould, Dorothy Palmer, Tommy and Dorothy Simpson, Margaret Myers, Ann Burton, Margaret Addyman, Tom Hird, Elizabeth Simpson, John Wilkinson, Maurice Dinsdale, Dane Swires, Eddie and Evelyn Verity, Gladys Spence, John and Joan Jefferson, Tom and Doris Carling, Brian and Hilda Smith, Ken Balsdon, Herbert and Pat Holmes, Cecily Helliwell, Alec and Beatrice Godley, Martin and Lorraine Whitley, Hilda Whitley, Margaret and Allan Hullah, Maud Marshall, Jean Morphet, David Lister, Dorothy Oliver, R Walker Barrett, Alister Wilkinson, Edward Brown, Marion Stockdale, Cyril and Joy Robinson, Graham Bell, Neil and Marion Richmond, Thomas Wood, Peter Jackson, Clive and Audrey Holmes, Jessie Norfolk Fred Skaife, Geof Blacker, Mike Gill, Geoff Raw, Peter Lee, Doreen Lee, West Yorkshire Archive Service, Bradford.

If you have helped in some way and I have omitted to mention you above, please accept my sincere apologies.

Some details of events have been obtained from old newspaper cuttings where the actual newspaper was not specified. Some photographs are known to have been taken by the *Pateley Bridge & Nidderdale Herald* who are thanked for their permission to reproduce here. Whilst efforts have been made to trace photographers to obtain permission to use their pictures, it is possible that some pictures may be from images produced by unknown photographers who cannot be acknowledged and consequently their names are not recorded.

Introduction

Amongst many varied memories of life in Nidderdale recalled by the current generation, or mentioned as being relevant to their precedessors, are: quarrying stone at Scotgate Ash; heavy horses ploughing at Pyefield; navvies toiling at Angram; clog-wearing children at Dacre School; building haycocks at Bewerley; a water wheel turning at Folly Gill Mill; attending the cinema at Pateley Bridge; shoeing horses at Clapham Green; the 'Pateley Flyer' steaming up the dale; worshipping at Birkhill Chapel; unloading hemp at New York Mills; and sheep washing at Sigsworth.

Just a few varied activities and events which were all once part of life in the dale stretching from Killinghall and Ripley through to Angram, now overtaken by progress and consigned to the past. Yet still they exist, not only in memory and account, but also in photographs spread far and wide across the dale. An individual photograph can tell us a great deal, but put together with others, its interest can be greatly increased. Together they can provide a fascinating and valuable record of times gone by.

My personal involvement with old photogaphs stems from time spent in Nidderdale's neighbour, the Washburn Valley, where an interest in 'How it used to be' developed, partly fuelled by a frustration that so much of historical and social interest had disappeared within the last century and could no longer be seen and photographed. As readers of my first book *Washburn Valley Yesterday* may recall, many old pictures existed, and it was whilst searching for and copying Washburn images that a few Nidderdale examples came to light. They were also copied, and so began a modest collection of Nidderdale pictures which has grown considerably over the past three years.

Many people in the dale have been very helpful — some especially so — not only in permitting their pictures to be copied, but in a variety of other ways, and without their help a number of slide shows held in the dale and the publication of this book would not have been possible.

As with the Washburn Valley, problems of memory and detail have been encountered. So if, on looking through this book, you find an inaccuracy, please understand that a genuine attempt has been made to be as precise as possible.

Due to the area covered by Nidderdale, the size of its population and the logistics of getting around to see enough people, the images here are merely a scratch on the surface of what pictures there may be within the dale. The book is not truly representative of, nor does it do justice to any area, or past activity. It merely puts together a small number of images which record a little of Nidderdale's recent past.

David Alred
Otley, May 2001

Pateley Bridge

A view of Pateley Bridge from a card posted in 1917.

The attractive High Street, Pateley Bridge, with its range of shops, accommodation and other well-advertised facilities being enjoyed by residents and visitors on a bright summer's day.

Amongst the many businesses in High Street are Wrays grocers shop, whilst on the right is Pudseys Hotel, café and confectioners, and a little higher up the Bay Horse and Black Bull public houses.

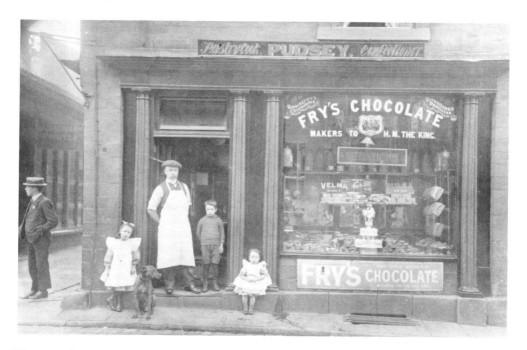

The shopfront and window display at Pudseys confectioners, c1916. The proprietor Mr Pudsey is in the doorway together with Bobby Pudsey. One of the girls is Frances Pudsey.

Pictured about 1910 outside the butchers shop of H Weatherhead & Sons, at the bottom of High Street, are John Weatherhead, Lloyd Layfield and Harry Weatherhead.

The shopfront of Wrays grocers and greengrocers in its original position well up High Street.

One of the occasions when flooding affected High Street, c1950s. A postman punts across, said to be on his way to the railway station to collect mail.

The bottom of the High Street badly flooded in summertime, 1954.

Two once-popular High Street inns, the Bay Horse and the Black Bull, pictured in the early 1950s prior to demolition, which, together with buildings at their rear, opened up an area subsequently developed as a car park and small estate of elderly people's bungalows.

Looking down High Street on a busy day in 1924. Perhaps it's Nidderdale Show day?

The old market hall on the corner of Colbeck Lane and Church Street, c1910. It was built by Thomas Carter Cameron, a retired grocer, as a large shop, and let in portions to traders.

King Street, leading up towards St Cuthbert's Church. Prominent on the left are the cinema built in the early 1930s and the board school, whilst on the right is the wooden hut where Jimmy Ross sold menswear, and a corner of the old feast field.

A scene in the Pateley Bridge coal yard, beside the North Eastern Railway sidings, as dalesfolk wait for their horse-drawn carts and a Thorneycroft flat wagon to be loaded with coal, 1924.

A view c1910 of the very busy sheep fair at Pateley Bridge. In the background is Bridge House Gate School.

Situated between Low Wath Road and the River Nidd, the recreation ground in Pateley Bridge, with its pavilion, bowling green, tennis courts and children's amusements, has proved popular over many years, both to residents and visitors to the town. In this photograph taken in the mid-1960s, the swings and slide are much in demand. On the far side of Low Wath Road, the old drill hall, Jack Longster's petrol pumps and the West Riding Yard are visible.

The bridge over the River Nidd viewed from a pathway between the riverbank and the North Eastern railway line.

Nidderdale Shows

Nidderdale Show was first held in 1895 in Pateley Bridge, and from a modest start has progressed to become one of the premier agricultural shows in the north of England. Its numerous events and classes provide many with an opportunity to compete, whilst for others it is an eagerly awaited social occasion — a day out not to be missed by many people from Nidderdale and further afield. The picture is of crowds enjoying an event at the 1905 show.

Joseph King, farmer and general haulier, proudly displaying his well-turned-out Shire horse and cart, c1950.

Isaac Oliver with a prize-winning cow at an early Nidderdale Show. His father, also Isaac Oliver, is the onlooker second on the right.

Ann Summersgill, Freda King and Audrey Summersgill with their Ayrshire and Friesian entries, in the cattle-judging ring at a 1950s show.

Joanna Dawson, Audrey Summersgill and Ann Summersgill, exhibitors in a Young Farmers Club Friesian calf class at a 1950s show.

A group at Nidderdale Show, c1945. They include: Bob Pearson, Freda King, Frances Verity, Joe Stoney, Willy Carling and Joan Ibbotson.

Exhibiting their Dalesbred sheep in the 1980s are Ellen Lee, Martin Brown, John Graham, Michael Brown, Jock Beecroft, Andrew Stoney and Keith Verity. Judging their entries is Maurice Bradley.

Sheep judging in progress at the 1923 show.

Jack Hollings of Old Well House Farm, Low Laithe, and a prize-winning shorthorn cow at a Nidderdale Show in the early 1930s.

William and Frances Ann Mudd of Slade House Farm, Thornthwaite, at a Nidderdale Show in the 1920s. Both served on the committee of the Nidderdale Agricultural Society for many years. They were also exhibitors of dairy produce. Mrs Mudd exhibited widely for over forty years, and by 1922 she had won 477 awards for butter, bread, eggs, hams and bacon. She and her daughters were noted for their highly successful displays of finely executed butter flowers.

Butter flowers such as these magnificent examples were sometimes exhibited at Nidderdale shows. Here, however, Phyllis Louisa Mudd (a daughter mentioned in the previous caption) is displaying a prize-winning entry at the London Dairy Show in 1927.

Ibbotsons of High Street, Pateley Bridge, with their vehicle and product display at Nidderdale Show, 1923.

The catering marquee of A Wilkinson of Summerbridge at a 1940s show. The ladies are Cissy Holmes, ?, Mrs G E Wilkinson and Mrs Carling, with Clarice Carling in front.

Longster Bros display of products at an early 1920s show. Note the board advertising a fourteen-seater charabanc service from Longsters Garage to Lofthouse for use by people returning to homes in the upper dale after their day at the show. Joe Longster is on the right.

A tug-of-war event at a late 1940s show. Participating are Fred Summersgill, Tommy Mawer, Peter Hanley, Frank Fieldhouse, Frank Suttill and Jack Hannam.

Donkey race, Nidderdale Show, 1908.

Geoff Walmsley of Haverah Park and later Scarah Bank Farm, who enjoyed show-jumping success at Nidderdale Show and elsewhere, pictured in the late 1940s with Silver Mint, Lazy Boy and Bobby, and a grand array of trophies.

Stewards in Victorian dress at the Nidderdale Agricultural Society Centenary Show in 1995: (*left to right*) Charles Grundy, Mrs Rose Grundy, Audrey Summersgill, Jack Haines, Don Calvert, Mrs Eileen Haines, Bert Cave, Mrs Sheila Cave, Fred Spence and Marion Anderson.

Whilst the Nidderdale Show, held in Pateley Bridge, is the dale's major agricultural show, it is not the only one. The annual Ripley Show attracts many exhibitors including Robert Sidney Smith of Birchwood Farm, Ripley, seen here with a Large White sow at a show c1960.

Successful exhibitors at a 1930s Ripley Show taking part in the parade of champions. They include Clifford Lister, David Lister, John Lister, Frank Steele, Eric Steele, and further back Frank Brown.

Children

There are many examples existing of annual school photographs. Here are just a few, beginning with Heathfield School in 1897.

Ramsgill School, 1903.

Summerbridge School, c1900.

Summerbridge School, c1948/9: (rear) Denise Beck, Margaret Swires, Elsie Bradley, Sheila Carrington, Emily Moor, Patrick Gratton, Albert Nelson, Ian Bateman, Michael Smith, Jim Addyman, Ken Balsdon, Gerald Mason; (front) Margaret Hastings, ? Procter, Margaret Moor, Elsie Storey, Janet Gratton, Jean Holdsworth, Sheila Briggs, Valerie Dawson, Betty Hardcastle. Teacher: Mrs Holmes

Children gathered at the rear of the council houses in Summerbridge in 1937: (*left to right*) Alan Holmes, Max Bentley, Doreen Dawson, Brenda Dawson, Margaret Bentley, Ken Holmes and Terry Proctor. In the background is Raymond Bentley's Morris Commercial lorry.

Gerald and Muriel Simpson taking lunch and a can of tea to workers cutting oats at Old House Farm, Fouldshaw Lane, Dacre, August 1941.

May Day fancy dress group at Dacre Banks, c1950. They include Gillian Dodds, Peter Dawson, Linda Emsley, Shirley Atkinson, Jill Taylor, Celia Baines, Kath Newbould, Susan Atkinson, Brenda Kirkbright and Margaret Swires.

Ripley School pupils at Ripley Village Garden Fete in 1951:

(rear) Julia Boyd, Shirley Bland, Joyce Ingram.
(centre) Peter Smith, Joyce Bland, Leslie Swales, Ian Reid.
(front) Barbara Harland, Helen Lishman, Jennifer Marshall, Gillian Reid,
David Thompson, Maureen Kelly, Gillian Bland, Priscilla Boyd, Kathleen Smith.

The Famous Five — five girls from the Scarah Mill Area, 1955: (*standing*) Faith Marshall, Joyce Bland, Shirley Bland; (*in front*) Gillian Bland, Jennifer Marshall.

Children enjoying a roundabout on a flooded recreation ground, Pateley Bridge, early 1950s; (*rear*) Trevor Lawson, Rosie Lambert, David Beckett; (*front*) Billy Hustwith, Gerald Beckett, Geoff Raw, Susan Fisher, Margaret Fisher.

A group of Dacre schoolchildren in 1905.

A second group of Dacre schoolchildren .

Audrey Mary Bland of Scarah Mill Farm, pictured about 1915.

Robbie, Winnie and Bernard Gill at Nidd View, Summerbridge, c1905.

General Scenes

The entrance to Brimham Rocks many years ago.

Gill family members beside the River Nidd at Dam Stakes, Low Laithe, c1905.

Yorke's Folly, Guisecliff. The three stoops were erected by local labour, primarily to relieve unemployment in the late eighteenth century. The benefactor was John Yorke, who paid the workmen 4d a day and occasionally also a loaf of bread. The right-hand stoop was blown down in a gale in 1893.

Cattle crossing the River Nidd at Summerbridge near the aqueduct which carried water from Low Laithe to New York Mills.

An array of early motor cars outside the Yorke Arms Hotel in Ramsgill. The gathering would be at the beginning of the grouse-shooting season. Picture from a card posted in 1907.

Lodge Farmhouse and Methodist Chapel, Lodge Moor, upper Nidderdale. In the 1920s the Simpson family farmed here, to be followed by the Wellocks, part of a small and remote community which included farms at Angram and West Houses. The chapel served a wide area, but a very small population, and is said to have had only twelve members prior to its demolition in 1929.

West Houses Farm, Angram, in pre-reservoir days, though a line of apparent workings across the hillside may be for Angram Reservoir's north bye-channel.

A street scene in Middlesmoor, including Richard, Mary, Martha and Jim Lee outside Dicky Lee's joiners shop, the school house and Middlesmoor School, and a few Lofthouse and Middlesmoor bandsmen at Bell Festival time. (See page 47 for details of the Bell Festival.)

Sandy Drummond pictured beside the water fountain which he built in Lofthouse in the early 1900s. On the right is John Stones' general store and post office. John Stones also worked as a leadminer.

A corner of Birstwith, featuring the water fountain. At one time this was the only supply available in the village for domestic consumption, using river water supplied by gravity feed to a well and then into the fountain. The allotments behind have since made way for more dwellings.

Thatch-roofed Jonathan Cottage in Birstwith.

Kettlesing Concert Hall. A centre for village social activities in the Kettlesing/Felliscliffe area, it was a converted ex-army hut which arrived in 1920 via Birstwith Station. Following installation, it was later fitted out with extras such as heating by coal stove.

A West Yorkshire Road Car bus negotiating the flooded road between Dacre and Summerbridge in the early 1950s.

Floods in the centre of Hampsthwaite on the 2nd July 1968. Along with much of Yorkshire, this area was affected by a violent storm which produced inches of rain and in some areas large hailstones. Hampsthwaite's roads were quickly awash, and nearby some bushes and trees had their leaves stripped and bark removed on the side getting the full force of the hailstones, which in some spots lay inches deep after the storm had passed.

Sarah and Wiliam Bramley at the Duke William Inn in the hamlet of Meggate, Birstwith, c1890s.

A scene on an ancient track on Dead Man's Hill, Angram, from a card posted in 1904.

A Greenhow scene featuring the Wesleyan Methodist chapel, which was built in 1775. Like many such chapels, it suffered fluctuating fortunes dependant upon the local economy and population figures. It eventually closed and was sold in 1948 for £265.

Winter weather problems at Greenhow, as efforts are made to clear a way through deep snow outside the Miners Arms. Picture believed to be from the early 1950s.

Blizzard conditions in Middlesmoor on the 30th November 1965.

Two days later.

Middlesmoor on the 2nd December 1965: Digging out the road to Lofthouse.

Martin Holmes and Glyn Griffiths coping with winter conditions in Moor Lane, Middlesmoor, on the 1st December 1965.

People

Social, Amateur Dramatics, Leisure, Sport

Darley Temperance Band of 1911 ready to board their vehicle to fulfil an engagement. The Temperance Band was formed in 1901 following the demise of the old Darley String Band, and some years later it became the Darley Silver Band. The band, whose first conductor was Redford Procter from Dacre, was in demand for agricultural shows around the district, for which in the early days it was necessary to hire a wagonette and horses for the journey. They played at annual village school fêtes, and at the Darley Hospital Sunday Event on Stocks Green, local hospitals benefiting from collections at this event and others at churches and chapels. They led the procession through Darley at the Annual Rechabite Band of Hope Festival on Whit Monday, and were involved locally whenever there were national festivals, coronations, peace celebrations etc, and at many other local events, performing in their uniform of blue, red and gold. From 1932, the band rented a room in Waller Square for their weekly practices. They kept going when many such bands disbanded, two members, Joe Furniss and J R Houseman, completing forty-five and thirty-eight years service respectively.

A procession passing Darley School, lead by Darley Temperance Band, early 1900s. It is believed to be a Whit Monday Rechabite procession, which, having toured the village, would have progressed to the Walker Lane cricket field, where there would have been fancy dress and sports entertainment.

Darley Silver Band, with some bandsmen from Summerbridge, at the opening of Darley Memorial Hall in 1947. Amongst those standing are Herbert Bradley, Charles Fawcett, Edwin (Ted) Houseman and Ronny Swires; seated include Tom Whitfield, William Abbott, Thomas Houseman, Arthur Fawcett, ? Nelson, George Houseman, Joe Furniss, William Houseman and John Robert Houseman.

Lofthouse and Middlesmoor Band, formed in 1914 by Thomas Bradley of the Crown Hotel, Lofthouse. Amongst those members depicted are: (*rear*) Cyril Hall, Ernest Calvert and Tom Whitfield; (*middle*) Thomas Bradley, William Harrison, J J Calvert, ? Browse, Carlin Eglin and Sam Eglin; (*front*) Arthur Calvert, ? Browse, G Whitfield, Gilbert Eglin and Rev H Minton-Senance.

A Sunday school group at Woodmanwray, the chapel in the garth, at Grange Farm, Heyshaw, Dacre c1900.

Sir Thomas de Ingilby was granted the right for Ripley to hold an annual market and horse fair by King Edward III in 1358; some 550 years later it attracted considerable crowds to the village.

Dacre Banks Feast, which featured travelling showmen's rides, stalls and other entertainments on the green and nearby field for three to four days each September, immediately following the Nidderdale Show. Buildings in the background include the Royal Oak Inn and a house from which Tom Irving ran his business supplying local farmers with their requirements. He is particularly remembered for his sheep dip.

Above: Pateley Bridge Boys Brigade c1945/6 outside the cinema.

(*rear*) ?, ?, ?, ?, Peter Chadwick, Dick Holbrook, Alan Richmond, Billy Holt, Gerald Fletcher, Clive Holmes; (*middle*) Brian Mann, Robin Chambers, ?, John Milner, ?; (*front*) Harold Lowcock, ? Walker, ?, Denis Walker, ?, ?, Laurie Cockburn, ? Holdsworth, Charles Cockburn, David Johnson, ?, Brian Brown, ?, ?.

Opposite: Dolly Rodwell leading a Shire horse and a children's float at a Glasshouses gala in the 1950s. As a child Dolly hawked coal around Pateley Bridge for Hawksworths, to earn coppers to enable her to go to the 'flicks' in Pateley Bridge. In later life she worked at the general store in Low Laithe and delivered newspapers around the district. It is said that on weekdays she would rise at 5am and walk from Low Laithe to Summerbridge, deliver papers round the housing estate and New York area, and return to Low Laithe in time to cook for the family. After lunch she helped in the shop, and at 5.30pm she took the evening papers on the bus to Glasshouses, delivering them round the village on foot. She then walked to Wilsill and on to Low Laithe. On Friday she did an additional round of Summerbridge in the afternoon with her *Nidderdale Heralds*. She retired from selling newspapers when aged sixty-four in about 1979. During her lifetime she was involved in and actively supported many activities, including being a governor of Summerbridge School. Dolly was well known for her generosity to local people who were unwell, visiting and taking in meals etc. One of the dale's real characters.

Lofthouse and Middlesmoor bandsmen leading the Middlesmoor Bell Festival procession in 1951. The band includes Tom Bradley, Laurie Coates, Arthur Calvert, Reg Lee, Albert Ashby, Harry Metcalfe and Reg Coates, accompanied by John Lee.

The Bell Festival is an annual event held to commemorate the installation of a peal of six bells in St Chad's Church, Middlesmoor, paid for by Mary Ann Barkwith in memory of her uncle, Simon Horner, a merchant in Hull, with family connections in the Middlesmoor area. The one-day festival, which began in 1868, comprises a procession through the village to the church, the ringing of the bells, a church service, children's tea and sports. A small legacy provided by M A Barkwith makes provision for the children's tea and games on condition that there are no rude games.

The Ripley Pageant of 1930. Its purpose was to raise funds for Harrogate Hospital. The pageant had four scenes: Edward III visiting Ripley in 1358 and granting a charter for holding a yearly horse fair; James I being entertained at Ripley Castle in 1603; before the Battle of Marston Moor in July 1644 and a few days after the battle; and Ripley Fair in 1660.

Bell ringers at Birstwith Church, New Year's Eve 1947. They include: Arthur Ewbank, Frank Grange, John Stockdale, Arthur Worsnop, Rev Brittain, Jackson Ewbank, Bob Morley, Chris Lofthouse, George Gill, Peter Ewbank, Frank Barker.

Darley residents and members of the Girls Friendly Society repairing camouflage netting in the vicarage garden, Christchurch, Darley, during the Second World War. Amongst those pictured are: (*standing*) Kathleen Leeming, Winny Brotherton, Dorothy Thackray, Evelyn Kent, Doreen Hardcastle, Olive Brotherton, Joan Dunn, Joyce Reynard and Mrs Castle; (*kneeling*) Jean Warrington, Margaret Kent, Alice Clarkson and Jean Lofthouse. During the war, spinning at local mills was commandeered for production of items such as parachute ropes, shell-box handles and netting.

A steam-powered boat being enjoyed on the River Nidd near Summerbridge. The passengers include Hannah and Joseph Gill.

An early twentieth century wedding group photograph. The occasion is the wedding of William Gratton and Florence Scatchard. The venue is Scarah Bank Farm, the groom's family home, and the year is 1904.

The family of John and Sarah King at Coldstones Fold, Greenhow Hill, around 1900: (*rear*) Harrop, Amos, Lot, John; (*middle*) William, Mary, Sarah Jane, Hannah Elizabeth, Clara, Ann; (*front*) Emma, John, Joseph, Sarah, Alice Maud.

The Hannam family at Gouthwaite Hall, c1885: (*front*) William and Mary Hannam; (*rear*) William Hannam, Eleanor Rispin (*née Hannam*) and Emmanuel Hannam.

For some time after the completion of Gouthwaite Reservoir, due to high water levels, the family were only able to occupy upstairs rooms at the hall. They later moved to higher ground at Gouthwaite House Farm.

William Hannam senior was the first keeper at Gouthwaite Reservoir.

Muriel and Olive Longster appearing in the Gilbert and Sullivan Society's production of *Patience* at the Old Oddfellows Hall, Church Street, Pateley Bridge, in 1929.

A *Dick Whittington* pantomime group at the cinema, Pateley Bridge, in 1954: (*rear, left to right*) Dorothy Longster, Ann Swires, Ruth Moore, Ada Marshall, Sandra Grant, ?, Pat Spivey; (*front*) Shirley Watson, Betty Swires, Sally Hainsworth, Valerie Faulkner, Edith Dean.

A Joybells Dancing Class group at the cinema, Pateley Bridge, c1950s: (*left to right*) Marlene Weatherhead, Paddy Marshall, Ann Summersall, Joyce Wilmot, Joan Busfield, Jean May and Shirley Swires.

After the Second World War, a number of events were held in Dacre Banks to raise money for village improvements, such as a shelter, toilets, alterations to the green etc. Pictured thoroughly enjoying themselves at one such event in the early 1950s are Ernest Dawson and Jack Gill. A comment overheard on the day was 'my, what a well-built woman'.

Summerbridge Drama Group performing at Dacre Village Hall, c1938. The cast are: Kathy Bonner, Jack Gill, Florence Boud, Ernest Powell, Doris Gill, Herbert Gill, Joseph Arthur Gill, Herbert Seed, Alec Mackintosh, Muriel Tinkler, Nora Abbott, Charles Atkinson, ? Hirst, Mary Gill and Edith Atkinson.

Dacre football team pictured in 1920s. They include: (*rear*) Richard Calvert, Wilf Henson, Raymond Bentley and Charles Smith; (*front*) Harry West, Teddy Richmond and Duncan Castles.

Birstwith Cricket Team, pre-1900. The only ones named are George Wood (*rear, far right*) and George Jackson (*front, centre*).

The players and officials of Kettlesing cricket team in the early 1900s: (*rear*) Frank Walker (umpire), Joseph Morris, John Robert Wilson, John Morris, Claude Harold Hare-Gill (secretary and treasurer), Alexander A Sutcliffe, Jeff Swale (umpire); (*middle*) Horatio Joseph Grange, John William Walker (captain), Ernest Weatherhead, Mark Thorpe; (*front*) Robert Darnbrook Snow, Bert Walker (scorer) and Jess Houseman.

Kettlesing had a cricket team for forty years, and only the difficulty of fielding an eleven in 1914 led to the disbandment of the club. They played teams in Nidderdale and Harrogate, and had quite a run of success. However, it was a long time before they heard the last of a game against Glasshouses, who put Kettlesing out for three runs — two runs from the bat and one extra.

Birstwith WI darts team, winners of the Womens Institute Darts Competition in 1990. They are: Joan Hunter, Iris Petch, Biddy Brown, Marion Stockdale and Gladys Bass.

Dacre mixed hockey team. c1938: (*rear*) Mary Patrick, Mabel Powell, Jessie Wray, Elsie Charlton, Ted Richmond, Raymond Bentley; (*front*) Joe Swires, Edwin Gill, Tommy Swires, Ronny Swires, Freddy Swires.

Pateley Bridge football team, 1951-2: (*rear*) Sid Heaton, Dave Harris, Don Cockburn, Frank (Bartram) Dean, Bill Jamieson, Bill (Wiggy) Williams; (*front*) Harold (Dodge) Holdsworth, Charlie Webster, Peter Spittlehouse, Peter (Matey) Reynard, Brian Parker.

Pateley Bridge junior cricket team, c1954: (*standing*) Norman Dean, Brian Weather-head, Harry Leeming, Douglas Raw, Keith Raw, Philip Dyson, Billy Williams and ? Pratt; (*seated*) John Garside, Melvin Hardcastle, Ian Chadwick, Carl Foxton and Ian Weatherhead.

Members of Bewerley Bowling Club at the pavilion, Recreation Ground, Pateley Bridge, c1930s. They include: Fred Swires, Bobby Pearson, Charles Swires, Frank Hartley, Dicky Bowes, Dave Lawson, Fred Spence, George Houseman, Albert Pearson and Jim Metcalfe.

Dacre Cricket Club annual dinner, late 1950s. Enjoying the evening at the Flying Dutchman, Summerbridge, are: (*standing*) Joe Hardcastle, James Gill, Fred Carrington, R H Newbould, Jim Brogden, A C Wray, Bill Houseman, Fred Swires, Harry Brogden, Harry Raw, ?, Stan Robinson: (*seated*) Wilf Hewson, Ronny Swires, Teddy Richmond, Alec Wray, J G Pullan, Herbert Henson, John Briggs, Harry Dinsdale, William Houseman. J G Pullan donated the Max Pullan Playing Field to Dacre Cricket Club.

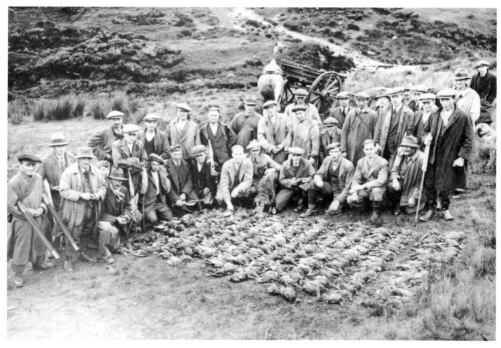

A shooting party on Lord Illingworth's Ramsgill Moor on the 13th August 1934, with a record bag of 410 brace of grouse shot in one day. Included are: John Smith, Alec Hudson, Fred Parker, Walter Rayner, Arthur Fryer, John Harker, Harry Metcalfe, Tom Dowson, Richard Metcalfe, Bob Kirkley, George Beecroft, Willy Harker.

Beaters were normally paid a shilling a day, but on this day received an extra shilling for the record bag.

A grouse-shooting party on Sigsworth Moor at the shooting box, c1912–16.

Sheep washing in Burn Gill, Gouthwaite, c1908. Washing usually occurred about the third week in June, its purpose being to remove sand, grit, grease and dirt from the fleece prior to clipping, which would follow about ten days later. Local men would enter the water, sometimes with their sleeve ends and trouser bottoms tied with twine in an attempt to keep their bodies warm whilst working. In later years, men became less keen to enter the cold water, and long-handled dipping crooks or sticks were used to push the sheep underwater. The practice of sheep washing continued in Nidderdale up to about the early 1930s. The sheepwasher on the right in this picture is Moses Rayner.

A few workers and many observers at a sheepwash at Stean in early 1900s.

Sheepwashing at Sigsworth in 1922.

In Nidderdale, sheepwashing was looked upon as a day out to be enjoyed and many local families would attend — some, particularly the ladies, often dressed up for the occasion. Food would be brought along for what became a big picnic on the hillside. The picture shows part of the gathering at Stean in 1907.

Another view of the sheep and crowd gathered at Stean in 1907.

Businesses
Mills, Shops, Transport etc

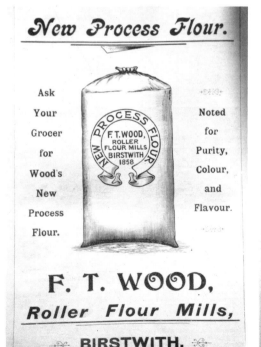

THE
Nidderdale Ales

ARE PRODUCTS OF

MALT AND HOPS,

AND BY REASON OF THEIR

Purity and Excellence

ARE WIDELY RECOMMENDED BY THE

MEDICAL PROFESSION.

PRICE LIST.

	Per Gal.		Per Gal.
Pale Bitter Ale (A) ...	1/8	Light Bitter Ale (XB),	1/-
Pale Ale ...	1/4 & 1/6	Porter	1/2
Mild Ale...	1/-, 1/2, & 1/6	Stout ...	1/4 & 1/6

In Casks of 9, 12, 18, 36, & 54 Gals. Carriage Paid.

BOTTLED LIST.

Half-Pints.	Per Doz.	Pints.	Per Doz.
Pale Ale (A) ...	... 2/-	Guinness's Ex-Stout ...	2/-
Extra Stout ...	... 1/9	Pale Ale ...	3/-
Bass's Pale Ale ...	... 2/3	L.B. Ale... ...	... 2/6
	Stout ...	... 2/6.	

John Metcalfe & Son, Ltd.,
Brewers and Spirit Merchants,
NIDDERDALE BREWERY,
PATELEY BRIDGE.

Three early 1900s adverts for Nidderdale businesses

New Process Flour.

Ask
Your
Grocer
for
Wood's
New
Process
Flour.

NEW PROCESS FLOUR
F. T. WOOD,
ROLLER
FLOUR MILLS
BIRSTWITH
1858

Noted
for
Purity,
Colour,
and
Flavour.

F. T. WOOD,
Roller Flour Mills,
BIRSTWITH.

Telegraphic Address
"SCOTGATE, PATELEY BRIDGE."

SCOTGATE ASHSTONE Co.,
LIMITED.

Quarries and Registered Office:

PATELEY BRIDGE,
Via LEEDS,

General Stone Merchants
and Quarry Owners,

SUPPLY ALL DESCRIPTIONS OF

YORKSHIRE STONE.

Landings and Flags, Self-Faced, Tooled, and Machine-Polished.

Tower, Spandril, and Astragal-Moulded Steps.

Headstones, Landings, Steps, Sills, Heads, and Coping, Tooled, Sawn, and Polished.

Sinks, Kerbs, Setts, and Wall Stones.

Staircases, Plain and Moulded, worked accurately to Plans and Sections.

THE SCOTGATE ASH STONE QUARRIES are three-quarters of a mile from the North-Eastern Railway Station at Pateley Bridge (fourteen miles from Harrogate), and, being the most extensive in the county, possess the peculiar advantage of a direct line connected with the Railway. The Stone being loaded into Railway Trucks on the Quarry Hills, avoids transhipment. Orders received by morning's post for Stone in stock can be sent off the same day.

R. LAWSON, General Manager.

Christopher Pullan's milk delivery cart at Hole Bottom Farm, Dacre.

George Houseman with an attractive milk delivery cart at Walker Farm, Darley, c1910.

Ralph Robinson's fleet of milk lorries at Brookroyd, Hampsthwaite, in 1951. Robinson had farmed at Clint, carted stone from Clint Quarry, delivered coal around Hampsthwaite, conveyed milk from farms to Birstwith railway station and later began delivering milk by lorry to the Leeds Co-op Dairy.

William Reynard ran a general grocers and small farm equipment and supplies business at Bridge House, High Birstwith. The business later passed to Willy Watson. This picture shows William Reynard and employees at Bridge House, c1906: (*left to right*) Willy Watson, Edwin Blakeborough, Richard Ellis, Wilfred Yeadon, William Reynard and Charlie Hammond.

Blacksmith George William
Stockdale at work at the Smithy,
Clapham Green, Birstwith.

Arthur Stockdale with his son John pictured in 1953 working in their smithy. In regular
use are fire, bellows, anvil, welder, tongs and hammers, in a business which had been
in the Stockdale family for over 100 years.

Another horse-shoeing picture, here outside premises of Todd Bros in Summerbridge, c1950s.

Wheel hooping at Todd Bros. A metal tyre being placed around a wooden wheel.

Robert Weatherhead's garage and taxi service vehicles at premises off Greenwood Avenue, Pateley Bridge. Pictured in the 1920s, the vehicles include Chevrolet, Minerva and Crossley models.

Pictured beside a Nidd Valley Laundry Commer vehicle are Charles Fawcett, Neddy Reynard and John Robert Houseman. The business had been started in the 1880s–90s by Robert Pullan, a farmer who was having difficulties making ends meet and started taking in washing to supplement his income, and for many years items had to be hand washed.

In the 1920s the business employed about seventy people, including drivers who would go out, originally with horse-drawn carts, and later motor vehicles, to collect washing left at receiving offices, including Guiseley, Otley and Harrogate.

Vehicles and employees at Pullans Laundry in Darley. These vehicles are a Commer, a Ford, two Morris Cowleys and a Jowett; and the men, Edward Reynard, Eddie Kirkbright, Jack Layfield, John Robert Houseman and Jack Reynard.

Hampsthwaite's corner shop, at the junction of Hollins Lane and High Street, in the early 1900s. Run by C M Moon as a grocers, provision dealers and post office, it had previously been the business of W Wilson. Clara Moon is on the right in the doorway. The premises were demolished during the 1930s.

The general store and corner shop in Birstwith, with its delivery vehicle. The proprietors are believed to be the Emsleys at the time this photograph was taken.

Darley Post Office pictured in the 1930s. Residents of Darley, Birstwith, Thornthwaite and Thruscross could register births and deaths here on two days a week with the registrar and post office proprietor J C Bradbury.

The Wellington Inn, Darley, a free house which later became a Tetleys pub. Beer only was available until 1953, when a spirits licence was obtained. When photographed, the majority of the premises was a dwelling. At the rear of the room on the right was a room where customers drank, the beer itself being drawn in a back kitchen.

The Lee family's joinery business and premises in Middlesmoor, c1920s. This business later became Lee and Holmes.

Ramsgill sawmill, run by Orlando Atkinson. Water which drove the sawmill wheel also drove the wheel at the nearby cornmill of Francis Suttill. When the mills closed down the wheel was taken to Gouthwaite Farm, the then residence of Francis Suttill (jnr), and was later passed on to the Bradford Industrial Museum. Picture from the early 1900s.

Ramsgill Corn Mill, built about 1640 and operated by the Suttill family for over 200 years until its closure in 1926. The mill was known far and wide for its excellent flour and feeding stuffs, and especially its oatmeal.

Francis Suttill, born in 1847, the eldest of a family of eleven, raised in a small thatched cottage in Ramsgill. The picture shows him at Ramsgill Mill on his mare Alice.

At the age of ten he joined his father in the family corn-milling business in Ramsgill, working a 6am–9pm day. By eighteen he was travelling weekly, and sometimes twice-weekly, by horse and cart, to markets at Leeds and Ripon. Though a shorter journey, travelling to Ripon was still hard and time consuming, the route being up the steep hill out of Bouthwaite and over Dallow-gill Moor, through Kirkby Malzeard and on to Ripon. A 5am start was usual as the journey took over five hours, but returning with a cart laden with eight sacks of corn took even longer. There was an alternative route, but this involved two tolls, one near Ripon and the other near the Half Moon Inn at Fellbeck, and expense had to be considered, charges at each toll being 4d for horse and cart, and 6d for the driver. His visits to markets continued for over forty years.

For many years, cornmills such as Suttills thrived in the dale, as practically all the farms from Dacre to Angram had ploughs, and farmers were growing their own grain crops for feeding purposes and supplying their produce such as oats and barley to be ground.

In addition to milling, Suttills had also farmed a considerable acreage, and when easier forms of transportation and distribution resulted in the demise of locally grown corn, the Ramsgill mill was closed and the family concentrated on farming.

Francis Suttill, a churchwarden at Ramsgill for twenty-five years, had strong views on religion and morals, and did not believe in working on Sundays. However, as the maximum useage of available water was particularly important in milling, and in winter time when cattle food was especially wanted, Suttill would attend Sunday evening church, have supper and retire early to bed. At midnight he would be up and out to run the mill's machinery for two to three hours until the mill dam was empty. By the time work commenced on Monday morning, the dam would have filled again, allowing more grinding of corn to take place.

He would regularly tell his sons to get their shepherding done on Saturday, so that there would be nothing to do on Sunday, and was quoted as saying: 'I'd rather bury my lads than see 'em go off with someone else's wife'. In summertime, if there was no Sunday evening service at Ramsgill, he would go in his horse and trap up to Middlesmoor, attend service and then go to the Crown Hotel for a port or two.

He was a member of the first committee of the Nidderdale Agricultural Show and a lifelong supporter.

A Ramsgill Corn Mill yard scene, c1924. Horse-drawn carts were a regular feature at the mill, though a Chevrolet wagon is a sign of the times. The picture includes Francis Suttill (junior) and Percy Webb.

Darley Mill and dam. Used as a cornmill with a new water wheel and housing said to have been installed in 1875, it eventually fell into disuse, before becoming a timber merchants' store and stabling for Shire horses.

During the 1920s it reverted to being a cornmill under the ownership of the Skaife family. At that time the dam used to store water obtained from Darley Beck was badly silted up, and had to be cleaned out by hand in order to restore a depth of water sufficient for cornmill requirements.

In 1965, Charles Skaife ceased operation and a scrap merchant took over, later to be followed by a market gardener who had his garden alongside the dam.

Fringill Mill and cottages, beside Heck Gill Beck, Darley. The mill dates from around the late 1820s and has always been water powered, but supplemented over the years by a steam engine, gas engine, diesel engine and an electric motor. In the late 1800s a cornmill was built alongside, and following a fire in 1900 the cornmill was rebuilt at double its original size.

The cottages beside the mill have weaving cellars, the inhabitants perhaps hackling and spinning flax in the mill, and then weaving cloth from its yarn in their homes.

The mill was originally built by Benson Skaife, but later passed to Thomas Atkinson. In 1875 it was purchased by Robert Skaife and has remained in the family ever since. Over the years, work at the mill and its products have been flax spinning, linen manufacture, hemp spinning and twine manufacture, agricultural merchants and corn dealers.

From the spinning and grinding acounts of R Skaife and Sons, the following may be of interest:

January 1896 wages for one week's work
To Mary Ann Lowther — spinning.

Days	M	T	W	T	F	S	
Hours worked	9	9½	8½	9½	9½	5½	wage 5/6

To Tom Bradbury — hackling 20 stone @ 4½d   wage 7/6

To John Jackson — warping 231 stone   wage 19/3

1897 Grinding — quantities

Week beginning	sacks	product	Week beginning	sacks	product
March 6th	80	J. meal	March 13th	56	J. meal
	2	Pea meal		3	Pea meal
	1	Oat meal		1	Barley
	1	Boxings		1	Split corn
	18	Rolled oats		3	Oats
	1	Rolled oats		2	Oats
				1	F. corn
				1	Split wheat

Other produce around that time were sharps (whole wheat husks ground up into meal) and linseed.

Eddie Verity at Fringill Mill spinning and twisting yarn of different ply together to make twine.

Folly Gill Mill and cottages, where Frederick John Atkinson ran his business of hemp spinning and twine manufacture from 1891. Atkinson, born in 1853, had joined his father's business, but in 1882 he set up on his own at Bishopton Mills, Ripon, and in 1891 came to Folly Gill. In 1912 he purchased Glasshouses Mill from J & G Metcalfe. Over the years he gained a reputation for the quality of his twines.

The production of twine involves a number of processes. The raw material is hemp, which, having been subjected to emulsifying, is passed over breaker cards to remove any unwanted matter. Further cleaning at a finishing card takes place and the first sliver is formed. A process known as drawing follows, in which fibres are straightened and the sliver becomes finer for spinning into yarn. The material can pass through a number of drawing frames dependent on the degree of fineness required. It then requires twisting, a number of yarns — possibly of varying ply — being twisted together. The result is then polished, and is ready to be made up into hanks or balls as the finished twine product.

Staff at Folly Gill Mill pictured beside its large water wheel in the early 1900s. On the right is the proprietor, Frederick Atkinson.

New York Mills, the Summerbridge hemp spinning and twine manufacturing premises of Thomas Gill and Sons, viewed from across the River Nidd.

In 1825, William Hebden of Braisty Woods built a mill in a field beside the river. In 1827, Francis Thorpe of Knaresborough rented the mill for flax spinning. In 1834 he purchased the mill and began building houses for his mill workers. By 1851 there were 315 people recorded as living in the New York area.

In 1868 Thomas Gill began hemp spinning in the nearby Washburn Valley at Low Mill, West End, extending operations in 1879 by hemp spinning and corn milling at Dacre Banks. Following his death in 1880, his sons continued operating from both premises. In 1888 they purchased the New York estate, pulling down the old flax mill and replacing it with new premises. In 1889 they stopped production at West End and operated only in Nidderdale.

The arrival of a new boiler at New York Mills in December 1905.

From 1812 there had been a corn and flax mill at Glasshouses. In the early 1800s, Kirkby, Gill and Grange (a partnership) were involved here with flax spinning. By about the late 1820s the Metcalfe family had taken over, and in 1912 they were followed by Frederick Atkinson, the mill passing out of his descendants' possession in 1971.

Much of the development of the premises and the surrounding area took place during the Metcalfe period, their flax-spinning business having operated in Pateley Bridge and Shaw Mills. It was started by Mrs Elizabeth Metcalfe and continued by her sons John and George, who were followed in a later generation by George junior. The Metcalfes greatly extended the premises to provide extra space for all the processes involved in their business. They purchased land in the area, provided cottages for employees, built a day school and chapel, and a reservoir. During its ownership by the Atkinson family, the mill was used for hemp spinning and twine manufacture.

A cartload of hemp at Nidd View, Summerbridge, destined for New York Mills.

At Glasshouses Mill, Ernest Dunn and a colleague are passing hemp over a breaker card. Hemp was grown in many parts of the world, but major sources of supply for Nidderdale mills were India, Italy and Chile.

The Atkinsons of Glasshouses Mill operated the rolling mill situated between Pateley Bridge and Foster Beck. Yarn was taken there to be finished off. The picture shows employees at work in the rope walk.

The huge iron water wheel at Glasshouses Mill. Production at the mill depended greatly upon this piece of machinery, from the period of Metcalfe ownership right up to the days of the diesel engine, the mill having skipped the steam age for its power. The wheel was twenty-five foot (7.5m) in diameter and almost as wide, and in its prime did 3½ revolutions a minute and was capable of generating nearly 300 horsepower.

Frederick Thomas Wood and Mrs Sarah Wood and family, including George, Edith and Gladys, c1900.

F T Wood was the second son of Thomas Wood, who in the mid-1800s had taken over a flour-milling business at Wreaks Mill, Birstwith, from the Greenwood family. After time spent milling at Bishop Monkton, F T Wood ran the family business at Birstwith.

Wreaks Mill pictured in 1904 with Woods employees and three horse-drawn carts heavily laden with flour awaiting departure. Baking of bread was part of the business until after the First World War, and the covered cart is likely to contain bread for local delivery.

Wheat which was to be milled into flour was imported from Canada, USA, Argentina and Australia, being transported from ports such as Hull and Immingham by freight train to Birstwith Station. Eighteen stone (114kg) NER grain sacks have been loaded on to this cart for the short journey from the station to Wreaks Mill. Only much later was British-grown wheat milled at Birstwith.

Drayman George Gill with horses Jimmy and Prince pictured in 1910, about to leave Wreaks Mill. The sacks are likely to contain bran, sharps or flour for delivery to customers, or to Birstwith Station.

A 1920s picture of a Woods steam wagon and employees including Walter Robinson and George Gill.

F T Wood & Sons' loaded steam wagons and a horse-drawn cart outside the mill, c1925.

Sack filling and weighing in Wreaks Mill.

Loaded carts from Woods Flour Mill ascending Elton Bank, Birstwith, c1900. With the leading cart is Mark Stott, a carrier who farmed at Ross Bridge; George Whitham is in charge of the second cart.

Scarah Mill near Ripley, a cornmill run by the Bland family from 1860. It was previously operated by Joseph A Ingleby who also had a mill at Pateley Bridge, which was where Richard Constantine Bland served his apprenticeship before taking over at Scarah. Following his retirement in 1905, the business passed to his sons William and Arthur, and then to a further generation of John Richard and Harold Bland.

From 1815 the mill was powered by stream water, a modern turbine being installed in 1950. French stones were much used, and the business specialised in the grinding of oats and barley, and the production of flour from the wheat brought in by local farmers. They gained a reputation for quality wholemeal used for making brown bread.

By the 1950s the mill was mainly concerned with the grinding of corn, and the manufacture of all types of balanced rations for cattle, poultry and pigs, with the aid of modern machinery and plant. The cattle food was transported to customers in three motor lorries, whereas years ago twelve horses had been kept for deliveries.

Delivery vehicles being loaded at Scarah Mill.

The family of Richard Constantine Bland and Mrs Jane Bland pictured at Scarah Mill House about 1890: (*rear*) Walter and Constantine; (*middle*) Mary, Sally and Maggie; (*front*) Arthur, Jane, Richard Constantine and William: (*reclining*) George.

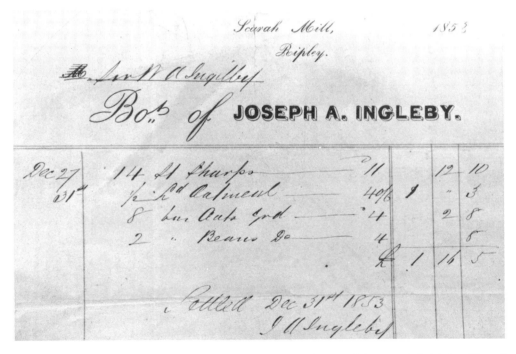

An 1853 invoice from Scarah Mill proprietor Joseph A Ingleby to Sir W A Ingilby of Ripley Castle for cornmill products, sharps, oatmeal, ground oats and beans.

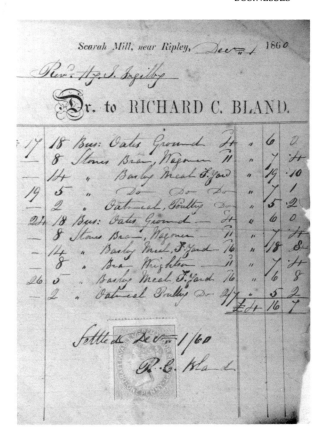

An 1860 invoice from Scarah Mill proprietor Richard C Bland to Rev H J Ingilby of Ripley for cornmill products.

Two months earlier, Rev Ingilby had cut the first sod for the North Eastern Railway line through to Pateley Bridge.

Michael Skaife and his driver with a loaded delivery cart outside 'Low Shop', Darley. He was a miller and general store keeper and farmer. Note the lamps on the cart. In the background on the right is the Prospect Inn.

The premises of Robert Skaife and Sons, grocers, corn millers and flour merchants, known as the 'Top Shop', in Darley. Beside the vehicles are Sid Whitley, Jack Simpson, Tommy Hainsworth, Robert Skaife, Jenny and Ben Skaife, John Robert and Polly Skaife. The heavily loaded vehicle is a solid-wheeled, blue-painted Commer wagon. The general store and shop is to the right, the buildings to the left and set back being used as warehousing for varied products such as sugar, currants and soap.

Two Commer vehicles, with family members and employees at Top Shop, Darley. Robert Skaife is beside the cab of the front vehicle, which has chain drive to its rear wheels (before the introduction of prop shafts). Benson Skaife is beside the second vehicle.

George Edwin Skaife, Tom Skaife, Ben Skaife and Marie Skaife beside a Robert Skaife and Sons vehicle with its load of hay, c1920.

A heavy load of trussed hay at Top Shop, c1930s, needing the pulling power of three horses, Prince, Dick and Farmer.

The humans are Thomas Hainsworth, Joe Leeming, Johnny Mallaby, Robert Skaife, Ben Skaife, Mr Helliwell, John Robert Skaife and a visiting rep. In front are Jenny and Polly Skaife, and a cow (name not known),

Walter Aldon's shop in Waller Square, Darley. Opened in 1903 as a general stores and cycle dealers, the business later became Aldons Garage and moved to premises opposite the bottom of Stumps Lane, Darley.

An Aldons of Darley charabanc. In 1919, Walter Aldon had a passenger body made for one of his lorries, on which trips were made to the seaside, and journeys to Otley Market.

Members of Bouthwaite Wesleyan Chapel on an outing to Richmond, c1920. Transport provided by Walter Aldon of Darley. Amongst those experiencing a journey of forty miles (65km) each way on those seats are: on vehicle, *front left* – Marian Metcalfe, and *far right* – Cedric Harrison and John Smith; on ground, *from left* – ?, ?, Sid White, ?, Everard Metcalfe, Lawrence Coates, Mary (Polly) Metcalfe, Mrs Carling, ? Simpson, Miss King, ? Simpson, Mrs King, ?, Mrs Suttill, Mrs Coates.

Joe Grange Longster photographed in 1913 age twenty-five years. In 1871 his father Richardson Longster of Bridgehouse Gate, Pateley Bridge, had founded a business running wagonettes and pony carts for trippers in Nidderdale. The business was eventually sold in 1934.

Joe was the youngest of ten children. He began driving in 1904 and formed his own business selling and repairing bikes, motor bikes and cars. At the end of the First World War he was joined by his brothers George Richardson Longster and William Elston Longster, the business becoming Longster Bros.

Over the years the business became major road passenger carriers in Nidderdale, operating both private hire and public passenger services, and goods carriers, building up a fleet of coaches, taxis and other vehicles.

Joe Longster and employees Mitchell Wynn, Tommy Simpson and Duncan McCallum pictured beside the petrol pumps at Bridgehouse Gate, c1930s.

Four Longster Bros coaches.

Longster Bros coaches and other vehicles on their busy forecourt, c1940s.

A 1920s view of the Longster Bros garage forecourt providing parking space for cars of visitors to the Nidderdale Show. In progress is a cricket match, a popular feature on show day.

Two Wrays Bedford coaches at Feast Field, Dacre Banks, c1947, with Alec Wray the business founder, Walter Chapman, Tom Carling, Tommy Carrington, Harry Raw, Jim Thackray and George Smith. At the front are Kathleen Brown, Andrew Wray and Jimmy Norfolk.

Lead has been extracted from Nidderdale for many centuries. There were a number of mines in the Greenhow and upper dale areas.

This group of miners are at a mine shaft entrance at Westhouse Farm, Lofthouse, and include a Bell, a Caygill and John Stones.

Stone quarrying at Hope Quarry, Dacre, c1907. In the early 1900s, Arthur Thackwray was obtaining stone from Hope Quarry for his showroom and storeyard on Kirkstall Road, Leeds. He quarried medium- to coarse-grained sandstone, suitable for use in engineering, pulping and glass-bevelling industries. Amongst his products were large pulping stones which were used to crush timber as a preparatory process in the manufacture of paper, and a wide range of grindstones.

Stone from a local quarry, perhaps Middle Tongue or Scotgate Ash, arriving at the area known as 'the dock' beside the North Eastern Railway sidings in Pateley Bridge.

Pictured in Dacre Station yard in 1923 are John Lambert, Jack Lambert, Granville Chadwick and railwaymen. Their load is a stone said to have originated from Middle Tongue Quarry, specially cut for pulping wood in the manufacture of paper.

Harsh winter working conditions in a Greenhow stone quarry, operated by Nidderdale Quarries Ltd, c1950.

The road repair 'gang' of Charles Johnson at work at Low Laithe, c1910. Johnson originated from Killinghall and later lived in Ripon, where he stored his rollers in a field off Whitcliffe Lane. Posing for the camera are: Bob Johnson, Charles Johnson on the roller, and Mick Newbould on the horse-drawn cart. The men with brushes and a spade have not been identified.

Charles Johnson of Killinghall standing in front of his steam wagon being used to pull Kings Removal Contractors containers. They are pictured in front of the Bay Horse Inn, Burnt Yates.

Thomas Kidd Stobbs of Castle Farm, Ripley in postmans uniform, c1900. Having collected mail at Ripley Station, he delivered to Clint, Hartwith, Summerbridge, Dacre and Darley. He supplemented his earnings by acting as a carrier, running a smallholding, tailoring and cobbling, and even haircutting. His wife Laura also brought in income through baking and cake icing etc, whilst bringing up six children. Stobbs was a regular preacher at local Methodist chapels, and for many years kept a daily record of his income and expenditure, which forms an interesting record of his activities, and the cost of goods and services at that time. Two typical double-page entries for January 1908 are shown opposite. The following are other entries of interest:

INCOME

Dressed chicken for Mrs Warman	0-2-9
Half years boot allowance	0-10-6
Sold pigs to Mr Bentley	1-10-6
Mending shoes for Bertha Hood	0-0-10
Mrs Abbot paid me for haymaking	0-6-0
Sold Jas. Gill 6 ducks @ 2/4½ each	0-14-3
Haircutting	0-0-1½
Received for making brides cake for Miss Gosling	0-15-0
Lead some bags of nails for J. Walker	0-0-3
Carried A Bradley to station	0-0-6
Good Friday overpay	0-5-3½
Procuring postal order for Mrs Parker	0-0-2
Fastening buckles of leggings	0-0-5
Received from Mrs Lovell for cheese	0-2-1
Received of Mrs Swales for 1 weeks milk	0-1-2
Carried Miss Trees coffin	0-0-6
Met Mr Wintersgills luggage	0-1-0
Sold 10 cockerils to J. Atkinson	0-10-0
Sold iced cake to Miss Payne	0-3-6
Lead 1cwt of coals for Mrs Wilson	0-1-3

EXPENDITURE

Box of herrings	0-1-0
Horse shod, hind feet	0-2-6
Trap licence	0-15-0
Toll for crossing Ross Bridge	0-0-3
Clogs repaired at Hallers	0-1-7
Bottle of Honey	0-1-0
Perambulator wheel tye at Aldons	0-1-9
Paid for weeks tea at Darley	0-2-0
1 gallon parafine	0-0-9
2 mouse traps	0-0-2
Half stone beetroot	0-0-7
Stone of sugar from Skaifes	0-2-8
Castor oil at Emsleys	0-0-6
Shaving stick	0-0-10
Paid Mr Jackson for stirk serving	0-2-0
Paid Mr Alsop for combinations	0-4-11
Sheeps head	0-0-6
Trap shaft repairing at Housemans	0-1-3
Cyrils railway fare to Darley	0-0-2½
Gallon of beer	0-2-0

NON MONETARY ITEMS RECORDED
Sow pigged 6 pigs
Went to Brown Bank Chapel
Received winter uniform trousers
Got hay up into pike
Cow calved, bull calf
11 ducks hatched
Gilt brought forth a litter of 8
In bed with influenza

Top and above: Two double-pages from T K Stobb's income and expenditure book.

Thomas Kidd Stobbs pictured in Darley on his post round.

Bernard Webster and passengers pictured in Ripon on Webster's Chariot, a public horse-bus in operation from about 1910 to 1930. The chariot was a dual-purpose vehicle carrying passengers and goods around the area, its main journeys being from Bishop Thornton to Ripon and Knaresborough on market days. Webster also drove a wagonette for local cricket team away fixtures, and had a hansom cab. He farmed for many years just outside Ripley, and later worked on the Ripley Castle Estate, and delivered coal around Killinghall. The picture dates from 1914.

Reservoirs
Gouthwaite, Angram, Scar House

During the latter half of the nineteenth century, the population of Bradford more than trebled due largely to its greatly expanding textile industry, and in consequence water supplies of considerable volume and reliability were required. That water was to come from upper Nidderdale.

Bradford Corporation's intentions were to have reservoirs at Gouthwaite, Haden Carr, High Woodale and Angram. In the event four reservoirs were constructed — Gouthwaite, Haden Carr, Angram and Scar House. Haden Carr, built in the 1890s, was only small and was subsequently submerged under Scar House Reservoir.

The first reservoir to be constructed was Gouthwaite, for which the contractor was John Best of Edinburgh, and work began in 1893 and finished in 1901. Gouthwaite was built as a compensation reservoir to provide water for local industry, eg various textile and agricultural mills lower down the dale.

In this view we see the east end of Gouthwaite reservoir dam wall-top, walkway and water control towers, all constructed of beautifully dressed stone, whilst beyond are numerous hay pikes in fields at Stripe Head Farm.

An early scene April 1894 showing navvies using picks and wheelbarrows digging out the hillside at the east end of the trench, above which the masonry dam wall was eventually to be constructed for Gouthwaite.

By April 1895 a deep trench had been excavated and was being infilled. This view above the centre part of the trench shows the extensive timbering involved.

In amongst the timbering and cyclopean rubble which forms the foundations of the masonry dam. The large stone blocks have been excavated in the nearby quarry at Wath.

Stone extraction work progressing in Springwood Quarry, Wath. Stone was loaded onto trucks which descended a railway incline to the working site.

Construction of the east outlet culvert, April 1896.

By March 1898, outer stone cladding was in place on the dam wall at its east end. This view is taken above the gauge basin looking west.

In the same month, work is progressing further west on a wing-wall trench in the vicinity of Gouthwaite Lodge, which continued well beyond the lodge to prevent seepage of water round the ends of the dam.

By May 1900 the dam wall is nearing completion, as a steam crane is being used to lower a cut stone into place on the top of a water control tower.

Top and above: About eight months earlier, exceptionally heavy rainfall caused the premature flooding of Gouthwaite Reservoir. On the 1st October 1899, rainfall of 2.04" (52mm) was recorded at Ramsgill, followed by 0.3" (8mm) on the 2nd, and a further 0.99" (25mm) on the 3rd. The combined effect was that the near-completed reservoir filled with 1,600 million gallons (7,250 million litres) of water in three days from the river and surrounding catchment area. The dam's overflow valves, whilst fully open, were unable to cope, and the contract workings were flooded. Equipment, huts and machinery were swept away. The two pictures show some of the devastation around the dam wall.

The old Gouthwaite Hall, built in the 1600s, pictured at the time of the flooding in October 1899. It was later demolished and much of its stone was used in building the new Gouthwaite Hall on land separated from the reservoir by the Pateley Bridge to Ramsgill road.

Angram Reservoir, situated below Great Whernside, is a mile (1.5km) long and a third of a mile (0.5km) wide. It has a capacity of 1,100 million gallons (5,000 million litres) of water obtained from a catchment area of 3,750 acres (1,520ha). With a depth of over 110 feet (34m), it is capable of yielding a daily supply exceeding 6 million gallons (27 million litres), which is conveyed to Bradford via the Nidd Aqueduct.

The dam wall is constructed of cyclopean rubble laid in cement concrete and faced with dressed stone quarried locally. It has a maximum height of 130 feet (40m) and a length of 400 yards (365m).

Construction began in 1904 and by January 1916 the reservoir was full, and the contract deemed satisfactorily completed in September 1916.

The ceremony of cutting the first sod at Angram in August 1904, attended by officials and dignitaries representing both the contractor, John Best of Edinburgh, and Bradford Corporation.

The large quantities of stone required at Angram were obtained from Rain Stang Quarry, pictured here.

Two views of men working amongst the cyclopean rubble, huge masonry blocks set in concrete, in the trench at Angram, 1910–11.

With so much material and equipment to be moved around the construction site, steam railway locos were much in evidence. This one is pictured in October 1910 shunting loaded trucks on lines downstream from the dam wall.

The workforce at Angram included Scotch and Irish navvies. In this group are Robert Drummond, Duncan Drummond, Charlie Moore, Denis Donoghue and Jock Rabbit.

It is said that, at the end of a week's work at Angram, many navvies trecked over the hill to Middlesmoor where they bought postal orders to send home to their families, and then went on to the pub for liquid refreshment, sometimes to be found later sleeping it off in farm barns.

This page and opposite:

Four views of work in progress on the masonry dam wall, two views from downstream and two from upstream. Note the cranes, each with supporting pillars attached to flat wagons weighted down by large stones, to stop the cranes toppling over whilst lifting heavy items. The first picture includes the bottom of a scaffolding tower with trucks below and a loco alongside. This tower is also visible in the fourth picture. It was downthe tower that aggregate descended to a concrete mixer at its base. Mixed

concrete was then loaded into the trucks. A Blondin Line which crossed the valley was used for aerial movement of materials over the workings, its wires are visible in three pictures. In the third and fourth pictures the buildings on the far hillside comprise workmen's dwellings, mission building, stores, engine shed and the end of the railway line from Pateley Bridge.

Angram and West Houses Farms were to become casualties of Angram Reservoir construction. West Houses Farm is pictured on page 33.

The scene here pre-1904 is of Angram Farm in the valley bottom surrounded by moorland. The infant River Nidd is visible flowing past the farm, shortly before being joined by Stone Beck.

Over a decade later in this view from the end of Angram Dam wall, the buildings at Angram Farm are slowly being submerged by the rising waters of the new reservoir.

Another view looking down the length of the reservoir, past Angram Farm buildings, to the dam wall, where some work is still in progress.

Angram Reservoir and Dead Mans Hill.

A view up the dale along the line of the rough track known as Scar Road, photo-graphed after it has passed Scar House Farm and shortly before it crosses Scar House Gill; it then passes Fry House and New Laithe before crossing the River Nidd near Haden Carr and then ascending the far hillside towards Lodge.

Land in the valley bottom, including Haden Carr Reservoir, was to be eventually submerged under Scar House Reservoir.

Haden Carr Reservoir, built by contractors Morrison and Mason, pictured in early October 1899 following the heavy rains which caused serious flooding at Gouthwaite.

Scar House Reservoir, which covers an area of 172 acres (70ha), with a maximum water capacity of 2,200 million gallons (10,000 million litres) and a maximum depth of 154 feet (47m), obtained from a catchment area exceeding 7,000 acres (2,835ha), its water reaching Bradford via the Nidd Aqueduct.

Commencing in 1921, construction took fifteen years to complete, the first three and a half years being taken up with excavation of the site, during which 460,000 cubic yards (350,000m³) of earth were removed. The riverbed was excavated to a depth of forty feet (12m) to provide sufficiently strong foundations for the mighty structure which it was to sustain. A further twenty feet (6m) was dug for the cut-off, or tongue, which prevents water seeping through the strata below the dam, and the hillsides at both ends of the huge dam wall were similarly pierced.

The dam wall is 1,825 feet (555m) long, with a maximum visible height of 170 feet (52m), and over 540,000 cubic yards (410,000m³) of concrete and masonry weighing 1 million tons were used. Equipment on site included 13 steam locos, 25 locomotive cranes and 3 steam navvies, and at the height of construction a manpower in excess of 700. The total cost of constructing Scar House Reservoir was over £2 million.

An early view of the dam construction site, looking down the dale. The foreground area in this picture eventually went under the concrete dam piers. Beyond on the right is the valve and screening chamber building at the mouth of Rain Stang Tunnel, part of the Nidd Aqueduct.

A Ruston Steam Navvy removing rocks and earth from the hillside below Scar House Farm, and loading it into a train of tipping wagons.

Carle Fell Quarry, from which stone used in the construction of Scar House Dam was obtained. The picture shows the various working levels served by locomotives and cranes. In the distance on the top level is the loco shed, whilst bottom left is the top of the incline down which quarried stone was lowered to the stone stockyard, stone crusher and stone-dressing plant at the dam site.

The stone crusher and concrete mixing plant dwarf the 0–6–0 saddle tank loco *Mitchell*.

Rising from the dam trench are some of the massive concrete piers which create much of the strength and bulk within the dam wall. The cranes working in the distance are electric, whilst the nearer two are steam powered. The latter were liked by their drivers due to their warm boilers.

Another view featuring those massive concrete piers.

Inspecting work in progress at Scar are Bradford Corporation dignitaries Aldermen Craven and Gadie, with Lewis Mitchell the waterworks engineer. Their names, together with those of other prominent Bradford Corporation officials and important British military figures, were used as names for steam locomotives working at both the reservoir sites and on the Nidd Valley Light Railway.

Some idea of the diameter of the outlet pipe at the bottom of the dam wall at Scar is given by this picture.

The original Scar House.

Scar Village, built to provide accommodation and all facilities for the workforce involved in the construction of Scar House Reservoir. Situated about 1,000 feet (330m) above sea level, its electric lights were supplied by hydro-electric power from Angram. Its facilities included ten hostels, sixty-two bungalows, hospital, bakery, school, laundry, shops, post office, concert hall, cinema, reading room, recreation room, canteen and church. It even had its own resident doctor.

The picture house and canteen at Scar.

A range of buildings beside the railway track at Scar. They include sub-station no 2, offices, stores, fitting shop, smithy and loco shed. A sawmill and carpenters' shop are behind.

In 1936, following completion of Scar House Reservoir, the numerous buildings in Scar Village were no longer required and were sold off, many to have further uses as village and church halls etc.

Two Washburn Valley workmen, Stephen Beecroft and Walter Brownridge came to Scar to dismantle two bungalows which were then taken to Norwood and put together to form the village social hall.

Sections of pipe required for the Nidd Aqueduct were transported by railway up the dale and then off-loaded on to wagons for a further horse-drawn journey to the pipeline workings. Here a section of pipe is being lowered by crane on to a wagon at Ramsgill Station.

Another section of pipe at Ramsgill, requiring three horses to haul it up the hillside to its final destination.

The transfer of water from upper Nidderdale required the construction of the Nidd Aqueduct, which due to the nature of the terrain uses a number of siphons to facilitate flow along its length of thirty-six miles (58km) to Chellow Heights, Bradford. Built during the 1890s by contractors Morrison and Mason of Glasgow, it was a considerable engineering project incorporating a mixture of pipework, cut and cover, and extensive tunnels through hillsides, as well as bridges across a number of gills, the Leeds–Liverpool Canal and rivers Wharfe and Aire. Illustrated is the aqueduct bridge across Blayshaw Gill in 1897.

Stone needed for various structures along the aqueduct was obtained from a quarry in the Blayshaw Gill area, and was transported, together with sections of pipe and other materials, across the hillsides of Upper Nidderdale on a length of narrow-gauge railway line operated between the Heathfield and How Stean area. The picture is of the line crossing Riddings Gill near Colthouse, Gouthwaite, in 1896.

A bridge carrying the aqueduct pipes at Ashfold Side near to the wheel used to power water-extraction pumping equipment in the Merryfield lead mine, 1896.

The Nidd Aqueduct bridge over the River Wharfe at Barden nearing completion

Construction work in progress on the aqueduct bridge at Cottingley, which enabled Nidderdale water to cross the River Aire shortly before reaching Bradford.

Railways

To facilitate transportation of equipment, supplies and workmen, John Best, the Angram contractor, built a three-foot-gauge light railway from Lofthouse to Angram, later extending to Pateley Bridge. In 1904 the Board of Trade agreed to this railway being standard gauge and it was replaced by Bradford Corporation's standard-gauge line from Pateley Bridge to Angram, and called the Nidd Valley Light Railway (NVLR). Formally opened in September 1907, this line became the first municipal passenger railway in Great Britain.

Planned in conjunction with Bradford Corporation's construction of reservoirs in the upper dale, it had been intended to be solely for that purpose, but in order to meet Board of Trade requirements it had to provide a public passenger service. Passenger and freight trains ran through from Pateley Bridge to Lofthouse, from where services were restricted to the carriage of workmen, materials, equipment and supplies only up to the reservoir construction site.

For many years the line provided a valuable service, linking with NER trains at Pateley Bridge. However, by the end of 1929, following a decline in profitable operation, passenger services ceased and the line was solely used for freight, until it finally closed after completion of Scar House Reservoir in 1936.

The picture shows 3' gauge loco *Angram* with a short supplies train.

An even shorter train comprising of the loco *Angram* and carriage *Kitty*.

XIT, one of John Best's locos pictured at Lofthouse.

One of John Best's pug locos in front of buildings at Angram, including men's accommodation, the mission building (with passenger platform at front), canteen with quarters above, and stores and shop.

On 11th September 1907, the day of the formal opening of the NVLR, an inaugural passenger train carried Bradford Corporation dignitaries from Pateley Bridge to Angram. Loco *Holdsworth* pulled the train comprising carriages and saloon car as far as Lofthouse, where two of John Best's locos took over. This picture is believed to be of that train standing at Lofthouse prior to departure for Angram.

The 0–4–0 saddle tank loco *Craven* in the stone stockyard at Scar House, during the 1920s.

Some trains carrying supplies were particularly heavy and provided a severe test for locos and crews, especially on the one-in-forty gradient between Lofthouse and Scar. In this scene just above the tunnel cutting, four locos are hard at work heading for Scar with what may well be a cement train. The locos are *Milner* and *Blythe*, assisted at the rear by locos likely to be *Kitchener* and *Watson*.

Assisted by a banker, loco *Gadie* heads a workmen's train towards Scar.

The 0–6–0 tank loco *Milner* simmering at Lofthouse prior to departing for Scar with a short train.

The NVLR station at Pateley Bridge where a crew prepare the 0–6–0 saddle tank loco *Blythe* for departure with a six-carriage passenger train.

The Pateley Bridge engine shed of the NVLR, with loco and steam rail car *Hill*. The properties on the hillside are at Silver Hill..

In 1937, following the closure of the line and lifting of the track, plant and equipment were disposed of by auction in Pateley Bridge. Lot 770 was a saloon carriage which had operated on the line since its opening in 1907. Painted maroon, it still clearly shows the Bradford coat of arms and the name Nidd Valley Light Railway. A sad but fitting reminder of a fascinating piece of railway history.

Dacre Station, on the 11½ mile (18.5km) single-track line of the North Eastern Railway from Nidd Junction to Pateley Bridge. The line opened in May 1862, the first sod having been cut in September 1860 near Killinghall Bridge by Rev H T Ingilby of Ripley. Passenger services commenced with four trains a day each way, later increasing to six, then seven by the mid-1920s, but by the early 1950s numbers were down to two a day each way. Closure to passenger traffic came in April 1951, but the line remained open for freight traffic until final closure in October 1964.

Pateley Bridge Station, one of six stations on the line, the others being Ripley Valley, Hampsthwaite, Birstwith, Darley and Dacre.

The loco may well be G5 class 0-4-4 tank loco number 1839, later renumbered 67253, which for many years was the loco in charge of passenger services on the line, referred to by some Nidderdale residents as the *Pateley Flyer*.

Farming

William Skaife with Daisy and Jewel at Pyefield Farm, Dacre, c1940s.

Percy Skaife and an assistant binding oats near Low Wood, Pyefield Farm, Dacre, during the 1940s.

Haymaking in a field opposite Summerbridge Methodist Chapel, c1905. On the right, holding a rake, is Harry Gill.

Taking a break during haymaking, Edric and Joseph Stoney rest against a well-covered sledge, as two horses are brought in by an unidentified man to pull the load away. In the background are many little haycocks in this scene at White Wood Farm, Bewerley, around the mid-1920s.

A stack being topped out with hay at Lodge Farm, Dacre, 1910. Those involved are members of the Houseman family, including Willy, Ada, May, William and Harry.

Sheep clipping at Whitleys, White Oak Farm, Summerbridge, c1900. The three men on the left are John Houseman, George Whitley and John Whitley, and on the far right is William Whitley.

Annie Edith Barras feeding her Shire horse Nancy and its foal at Darley, c1925–30.

Joseph Emsley and Harry Moyses leading corn at Fellbeck in 1923.

John Mawer on Ferguson tractor at Broomfield, Wath, pulling a load of hay on a sledge.

Ronny Jackson and Scott Lumley with tractor and binder at Fellbeck House, c1939–45.

Mary Suzannah (Polly) Skaife feeding geese and hens at Field House, Darley.

Baling hay at Bridge House Farm, Wilsill, c1950s. Arranged around the Bamford Bailer are: Ethel Dale, Sam Hesselden, Jim Smith and Clifford Baxter.

Edwin Knightson chain-harrowing grass at Bungalow Farm, Clint, c1958.

Grass cutting in progress at Bewerley Home Farm. Operating the two-horse grass mower is Harry Summersgill, and standing beside him is Janet Summersgill, c1940s.

Everard and John Walker starting their first baler in the back field at Blayshaw Farm, Lofthouse, July 1969.

Levi Verity clipping sheep at Ruscoe Farm, Middlesmoor, c1940s, with Thomas Hird, Connie Hird, John Clark, Horace Thomas and George Verity. Looking on at the front are three wartime evacuees, Steve, Suzannah and Mary Pearce.

Harry Moyses scything corn
at Fellbeck House, late 1920s

Edric Stoney leading bracken on an iron-wheeled sledge at White Wood Farm,
Bewerley, in the early 1930s. The bracken would be used for animal bedding.

Raking up hay remnants from pikes, at the end of a haymaking day at High Sykes, Lofthouse, in the 1930s are Joss (George) Rayner, Maurice Hannam, Joseph Metcalfe and Mary Metcalfe.

Harvest field scene at Birchwood Farm, Ripley, 1926: (*far left*) Sydney Smith, then Robert Smith; (*driving tractor*) Ernest Smith; (*far right*) Annie Hayes.

Ronald Moyses driving a Ford pick-up carrying milk churns at Fellbeck House, c1950s. Harry Moyses bought the Ford, a 1928 Model A car, from a breaker's yard in 1938 for £5. The saloon body was then modified into an open pick-up and used to do practically every job a vehicle could do on his seventy-acre (28ha) mixed farm at Fellbeck — haymaking, cutting grass, carrying sheep and dung spreading etc. The only job it couldn't do was ploughing.

James Ernest Gill of Dacre with his Shire or Clydesdale stallion named Rocket. He is displaying and exercising the horse in Pateley between the bridge and the bottom of Greenhow Hill, in order to persuade onlookers to have their mares sired by Rocket.

Threshing day at Park House, Warsill, 1924.

Pictured at Birch House Farm, South Stainley, Groves Threadgold trims turnips as John Threadgold loads their cart, drawn by the Shire horse Daisy, c1960.

Sheep clipping at Lofthouse Sports, c1956. Bobby Lee and William Verity are clipping. Watching are Bob Busfield, Ernest Wood, George Beecroft, Sam Glencorse, John Harker, John Joy and Everard Walker.

Cattle judging at Felliscliffe Young Farmers Club Show, c1948. Present are Jim Brotherton, Fred Summersgill, Bill Scruton, Cynthia Armitage, Don Parker, ? Armitage, ? Kendal, Peter Heptinstall (judging), ? Todd, Edward Brown and Nora Tinkler.

Participants at a Felliscliffe Young Farmers Club ploughing match, c1948–9. Gathered round a standard Fordson tractor are: (*left to right*) Peter Grant, George Hullah, Eric Gill, Ben Hardcastle, Maurice Wilson, Fred Wilkinson, Charlie Hullah, Willy Clark, Nigel Clark, Ken Hornshaw and Allan Hullah.

Felliscliffe Young Farmers Club rabbit pie supper at Felliscliffe Village Hall, c1950s: (*left to right*) Rose Hardisty, Kathleen Hardcastle, Mary Tinkler, Mary Tinkler, Jean Wilkinson, Nora Tinkler and ? Armitage.

Jack Hollings of Old Well House Farm, Low Laithe, with horse and foal, in the late 1930s.

Lucy Emsley feeding lambs at Fellbeck House, late 1920s.

A budding farmer, Betty Stoney has her hands full at White Wood Farm, Bewerley.

Edgar Darnbrook of Croft Farm, Killinghall, and Victor Houseman, accompanied by Roy Curtiss, move their last two loads of loose hay, before balers came into use. Pictured about 1945, they are at the junction of Lund Lane and Otley Road, Killinghall.

Victor Houseman was known as an excellent stacker. He would fold over every forkfull of hay when constructing a load on a cart. All corners would be tied in by the next forkfull, and the load would be roped front to back, rather than side to side.

Jack Suttill at Ivy House Farm, Pateley Bridge, in 1957. Jack was a very successful competitor over a long period at sheepdog trials, here with his dogs Hemp, Jaff, Wylie and Jess.

John Threadgold with two Shires and a Clydesdale, Captain, Daisy and Monty, ploughing for roots (turnips and kale) at Birch House Farm, South Stainley, in March 1949. Beyond the gate and hedge on the far left are corn stacks thatched with wheat straw.

Dogs are very much a part of the Nidderdale agricultural scene. Here are two belonging to Alan Firth and Tom Whitfield pictured at Northside Head Farm, Middlesmoor, in October 1970.

Finally a dog at Scar brings to an end this look at *Nidderdale Yesterday*.